Anxiety In My Body

by Jordan Long, LMFT

©2024 Jordan Long, LMFT. All rights reserved. No part of this publication may be reproduced, distributed, or transmitted in any form or by any means, including photocopying, recording, or other electronic or mechanical methods, without the prior written permission of the author, except in the case of brief quotations embodied in critical reviews and certain other noncommercial uses permitted by copyright law.

ISBN: 979-8-35098-617-4 Hard Cover

ISBN: 979-8-35098-618-1 eBook

Dear readers,

My name is Jordan, and I am a therapist in California. As a therapist, I help kids just like you who are struggling with anxiety! I know firsthand how scary and confusing anxiety can be because I deal with it myself. My anxiety first showed up as many physical symptoms, and I spent a lot of time at my doctor's office trying to figure out what was wrong. When doctors kept telling me that my body was normal, I finally went to a therapist.

With this therapist I learned about the fight, flight, or freeze response, how anxiety can produce physical symptoms, and how my mind and my body were connected – information that I had never heard before from loved ones, teachers, or doctors. When my knowledge of how anxiety affects the body grew, as well as my army of coping tools, my physical symptoms started to disappear. They still pop up from time to time, but I can now manage them, and they do not feel as scary. The mind-body connection is amazing! If you are feeling strange sensations in your body, you should always get a checkup at the doctor first.

My mission is to educate kids about the mind-body connection, specifically how anxiety can affect us physically, and how we can calm our bodies by calming our minds. Awareness is the first step towards relief. I fully believe that if I had more knowledge when I was your age about anxiety, I would have had a lot less fear and suffering. I hope this book empowers you to talk about how your body feels, ask for help, and know that you are not alone when anxiety is in your body.

Love, Jordan

When there's a worry in your head
that you can't get out...

When you want to
run, hide, cry, and shout...

...this could be called "anxiety."

Anxiety can look like....

Your heart is **pounding** fast like a drum.
You all of a sudden want to get up and **run**.

You feel hot, like you just got out of the shower.

You want to have fun, but you just don't have the power.

Your body feels **shaky** as if you are shivering in the cold.

Your hands are so **sweaty** – there's nothing you can hold!

It's like you just spun around in circles – your head feels so dizzy!

Your mind is filled with so many things that it feels like it will always be busy.

You have trouble falling asleep, **tossing and turning** all night.

You get a strange feeling like you can't **breathe** right.

Your muscles feel **tight** and **sore** like you just ran a race.

You get a flush of **color** and **warmth** on your face.

Your tummy feels **flip-flopped** and upset. You feel like you are **swaying** on a boat – be careful, don't get wet!

Your lungs feel like they can never get enough air.

You can't focus on tasks, but it's not because you don't care!

Your fingers and toes feel tingly and far apart. You feel like there is a rubber band around your heart.

When you have these **feelings** in your body, tell a loved one first, and then go to the doctor.

They will do a routine **checkup** from your nose to your toes, to your trusty ticktocker!

When the doctor says that your body is healthy, they may ask you about upsetting **thoughts** and big **feelings** such as worry, stress, and fear.

When these thoughts and feelings are present, anxiety is likely near.

Anxiety is there to make sure that if there is a **danger** nearby, you are **protected**.

And the body sensations prove that your thoughts, feelings, and body are all **connected!**

But sometimes anxiety gets CONFUSED and comes when there is no danger.

And your body can react the same as if there is a

scary bear,

runaway train,

or creepy stranger.

Luckily, there are **skills** you can use to lower the anxiety and help your body **relax**. The first is telling yourself, "These feelings are just anxiety, I am **safe** – and that is a fact!"

Next, you can take deep breaths....
In for three counts and out for four.

Or pay attention to your "five senses" ...
Name 5 things you can see
Name 4 things you can touch
Name 3 things you can hear
Name 2 things you can smell
Name 1 thing you can taste

You can listen to music, read, or go outside – anything to help you feel **calm** and **clear**.

You can always tell a loved one what you are feeling – they will **support** you and they want to hear!

You can **talk** to a professional who understands, called a therapist.

This person **listens** to your feelings and helps you learn skills to calm your anxiety – they really are the best!

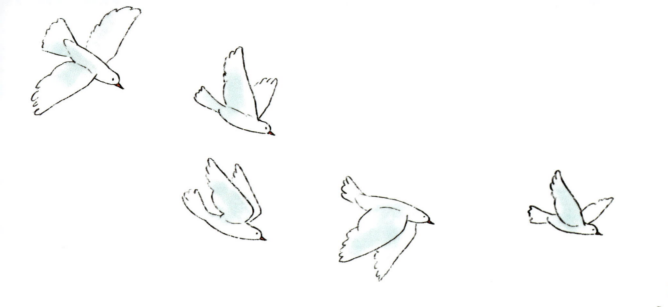

Nothing is wrong with you when there is anxiety in your body,

It happens all the time, everywhere, and to **everybody**!

Remember that anxiety will pass, and your body is fine.

When you share your feelings and use your skills, you can get through **any** tough time.

The Where's, Why's and How's of Anxiety's Physical Symptoms

Read and discuss with a trusted adult

As you have just read, the physical symptoms of anxiety can be terrifying, uncomfortable, and confusing, but you have the power to do something about them! It is helpful to know not only what the symptoms are, but also, why they happen and where they come from. Education is the first step in calming your mind and body when anxiety arises.

Anxiety is a biological response whose purpose is to protect us from a potential danger or threat. When a danger is perceived by your brain, your brain activates the protective part of the brain called the amygdala (ah-mig-dah-la), and the amygdala responds by enacting the "fight, flight, or freeze" anxiety response. This response is where the physical symptoms come from and are driven by hormones called cortisol and adrenaline.

However, the challenge comes when there is no actual danger or threat to you, but your body and mind react like there is. If you have the same anxiety response while watching TV or seeing friends that you would to a big bear looking at you like you are a snack, it sounds like anxiety is disrupting your life, and you may need support.

Since anxiety is your brain's perception of a threat, to lessen the physical symptoms, we need to send signals of safety and calm to your brain. The main methods to calm your body and your mind from anxiety are mindfulness and cognitive behavioral therapy (CBT). Mindfulness includes deep breathing, meditation, coping skills, and anything that brings your awareness to the present and reduces stress. Mindfulness sends a message to your amygdala that you are safe and that it is okay to calm down. CBT helps to explore connections between thoughts, feelings, and behaviors. It also helps to challenge distorted or negative thinking. CBT teaches us that our thoughts have a lot of power and can affect our bodies. A therapist is a great person to help you learn mindfulness skills and challenge negative thinking. Also, ask your parents, teachers, and other loved ones if they have any tips to manage anxiety.

The following is a breakdown of the physical symptoms that are mentioned in this book.

Fight, Flight or Freeze Response

- *"When you want to run, hide, cry, and shout."* Page 3
- *"You all of a sudden want to get up and run."* Page 6

These quotes refer directly to the "fight, flight, and freeze" anxiety response that is generated by the amygdala. The goal of this response is to protect yourself from a perceived danger or threat. The fight reaction is when your body chooses to react aggressively to a danger. This can look like shouting, screaming, hitting, kicking, stomping your feet, or saying mean words. Flight is when your body reacts by wanting to escape the situation. This can look like running away, leaving the situation, avoiding, or feeling fidgety or restless. And freeze is when your body and mind feel like it can't move or make decisions. With freeze, your brain can shut down or go blank, your body feels stuck or numb, or you have difficulty completing tasks. The fight, flight, and freeze response is the driver of all the other symptoms mentioned in this book.

Heart Palpitations

- *"Your heart is pounding fast like a drum."* Page 6

Heart palpitations are the feeling of your heart beating very fast, hard, or fluttering. When anxiety arises, your brain sends a surge of adrenaline which increases heart rate and blood pressure. This happens because if you were trying to get away from something dangerous, your heart would need to pump blood faster to get your body ready to react and engage in fight, flight or freeze to protect you.

Worry, Thought Spiral, and Lack of Focus

- *"When there's a worry in your head that you can't get out."* Page 2
- *"Your mind is filled with so many things that it feels like it will never be less busy."* Page 9
- *"You can't focus on tasks, but it's not because you don't care!"* Page 13

Usually, the most common indicators of anxiety are worries and thought spirals. Most people think that this is all of what defines anxiety but, as you now know, that is not true. Anxiety affects our minds and bodies. However, the physical symptoms typically start because of these worries and thought spirals. Worries can come up during a specific situation, when a life event is happening, or they can have no real reason at all. Thought spirals refer to a lot of thoughts going through your head all at once, and usually involve some sort of catastrophizing (thinking about the worst-case scenario). When your head is full of worries and thoughts, it is often difficult to focus on day-to-day tasks and enjoy life.

Body Temperature Rises, Sweating, and Face Redness

- *"You feel hot, like you just got out of the shower."* Page 7
- *"Your hands are so sweaty– there's nothing you can hold!"* Page 8
- *You get a flush of color and warmth on your face."* Page 11

The symptoms of sweating or body temperature rising are due to the surge of adrenaline and cortisol that goes through the body when the fight, flight or freeze response is activated. It is a similar concept when you exercise. With exercise, the hormones adrenaline, cortisol, and others, go through your body which cause your body to heat up, sweat, and get red or flushed. Your blood flow increases which is the reason for the face redness and warmth. When anxiety is present, your body wants to increase your internal temperature and hormone flow to get your muscles and organs ready to protect you from a danger.

Chest Tight, Shallow Breathing, and Hyperventilation

- *"You get a strange feeling like you can't breathe right."* Page 10
- *"Your lungs feel like they can never get enough air."* Page 13
- *"You feel like there is a rubber band around your heart."* Page 14

The sensation of hyperventilation (breathing fast and shallow), feeling that you cannot breathe, or having chest tightness are some of the scariest symptoms of anxiety. Usually these are the symptoms that we think of happening during a panic attack (a heightened anxiety response). During the fight, flight, or freeze response, your body wants to increase the amount of oxygen in your body, and lower the amount of carbon dioxide, to prepare for survival, which is why breathing feels off. Your chest and throat can also feel tight because the muscles there are preparing for fight, flight, and freeze.

Dizziness, Swaying, Numbness and Tingling

- *"It's like you just spun around in circles – your head feels so dizzy!"* Page 9
- *"You feel like you are swaying on a boat - be careful, don't get wet!"* Page 12

- *"Your fingers and toes feel tingly and far apart."* Page 14

As you have already learned, when anxiety is present your heart rate and blood flow can increase, and you can feel like you are hyperventilating or unable to get enough air. This lack of oxygen and increased blood flow to the brain can cause a sensation of dizziness or swaying. Sometimes, anxiety can also cause your blood pressure to suddenly drop which can also cause dizziness, the feeling of swaying or being unbalanced and sometimes fainting. Because blood flow is dysregulated and moving towards your core to protect your main organs, you may feel numbness or tingling in your fingers or toes.

Fatigue and Insomnia

- *"You want to have fun, but you just don't have the power."* Page 7
- *"You have trouble falling asleep, tossing and turning all night."* Page 10

Fatigue (tiredness) and insomnia (inability to sleep) sound like opposites, but they both can occur when anxiety is present. Fatigue happens because the rush of hormones causes our bodies to feel depleted. In fight, flight, or freeze, our bodies are working very hard to gear up to protect us and the constant action is exhausting. Insomnia usually occurs because you are having so many anxious thoughts racing through your mind that it is difficult to fall asleep or stay asleep.

Shaking or Tense Muscles

- *"Your body feels shaky as if you are shivering in the cold."* Page 8
- *"Your muscles feel tight and sore like you just ran a race."* Page 11

These symptoms refer to muscle tightness, or muscles tensing up when anxiety is present. If there is a danger, or perceived danger, your muscles contract to protect you from injury or pain and get you ready to fight, flight, or freeze. This muscle contraction can cause the sensation of shaking or trembling, as well as the hormones cortisol and adrenaline flooding your body.

Nausea and Stomach Problems

- *"Your tummy feels flip-flopped and upset."* Page 12

The symptoms of nausea and stomach problems with anxiety happens because of the surge of hormones and chemicals during the fight, flight, or freeze response. The hormones get into your gut and can cause nausea, constipation, diarrhea, or throwing up. The well-known saying "you have butterflies in your tummy" is an indicator of how the stomach is affected with anxiety. The gut is the largest endocrine organ, meaning that it is the largest producer of hormones in the body. Because of this, when anxiety is running rampant and causing imbalanced hormones, increased blood flow, and breathing dysregulation, it is only natural that your tummy may have some problems, too.

REMIND YOURSELF...

All these symptoms are one hundred percent natural and normal reactions that your body has in the face of anxiety. They are scary when you don't know why they happen. But now that you know, I hope it feels less scary. Your body is just doing its job by protecting YOU! By calming your mind, you can calm your body. You have the power to lower your anxiety.

Reference sources:

-Mayo Clinic

-Harvard Health

-National Institute of Mental Health

National Mental Health Resources for Youth:

Kids Mental Health Foundation
www.kidsmentalhealthfoundation.org

Children's Mental Health Matters
www.childrensmentalhealthmatters.org

National Alliance on Mental Illness (NAMI)
https://www.nami.org/Your-Journey/Kids-Teens-and-Young-Adults/

Never A Bother
www.neverabother.org

BrightLife Kids (California)
www.hellobrightline.com/brightlifekids

Author's Note

Thank you to all who have supported me in this dream of making a children's book. This book has been on my mind and heart ever since I began my therapy career, and it is finally real! A special shoutout to my husband, parents, family, and friends who always encourage me to follow my dreams and support me unconditionally. Thank you to my Aunt Debbie for your amazing editing capabilities and unwavering support, to Natasha Gunathilaka who created the beautiful and meaningful illustrations, and Amazon Publishing for making this book come to life. And last but certainly not least, thank you to every incredible person who has given me the honor of supporting them through their most vulnerable time. This book is for you.